FIGHT FOR
THE UNDERWO

HEL

VS

PERSEPHONE

by Lydia Lukidis

CAPSTONE PRESS
a capstone imprint

Published by Capstone Press, an imprint of Capstone.
1710 Roe Crest Drive, North Mankato, Minnesota 56003
capstonepub.com

Library of Congress Cataloging-in-Publication Data is available
on the Library of Congress website
ISBN: 9781669016427 (hardcover)
ISBN: 9781669016373 (paperback)
ISBN: 9781669016380 (ebook PDF)

Summary:
Who will become the queen of the underworld? Norse goddess Hel watches over the souls of those who die of sickness or old age. Meanwhile, Greek goddess Persephone can communicate with the dead and represents the change of the seasons. If these two goddesses clashed, who would come out on top?

Editorial Credits
Editor: Aaron Sautter; Designer: Bobbie Nuytten; Media Researcher: Rebekah Hubstenberger; Production Specialist: Whitney Schaefer

Image Credits
Alamy: Chronicle, 17, Ivy Close Images, 7, 10, Michelle Bridges, 25, NMUIM, 12-13; Art Resource: NY/bpk Bildagentur, 15; Dreamstime: Komposterblint, 5, 29; Getty Images: duncan1890, 22, Fine Art Photographic/John Collier, 21; National Gallery of Art: Corcoran Collection (Gift of William Wilson Corcoran), cover (bottom right); Shutterstock: delcarmat, 9, kaiwut niponkaew, cover (top left), 4, 28, Marta Cobos, 27, Warm_Tail, 19

All internet sites appearing in back matter were available and accurate when this book was sent to press.

Printed and bound in China. PO5379

TABLE OF CONTENTS

Words in **bold** are in the glossary.

TWO GODDESSES OF THE UNDERWORLD

CLING! CLANG!

The sound of clinking swords echoes across the river. Thick walls surround the water in this dark place. Welcome to the icy underworld.

Hel rules here. She's goddess of the dead in Norse mythology. Half of her face and body is beautiful. But the other half is just rotting skin and bones.

Hel

Who could possibly compete with Hel? Perhaps another goddess of the underworld! Persephone is from the **pantheon** of Greek gods. She spends part of the year in the gloomy underworld. There, she rules as goddess of the dead. She spends the rest of the year on Mount Olympus. There, she's the goddess of springtime, agriculture, grain, and **fertility**.

Which of these goddesses of the dead is more powerful? Who has more abilities? Hel and Persephone will have to fight it out to be the queen of the underworld!

Persephone

Hel comes from a pretty dangerous family. She's the daughter of the trickster god Loki and the giantess Angrboda. The wolf Fenrir and the serpent Jormungand are her **siblings**.

Loki and Angrboda kept their children a secret for a while. But the Norse gods eventually learned about them. They heard a **prophecy** that these monstrous children would grow up and cause problems.

Odin, the leader of the Norse gods, took action. He cast the serpent Jormungand into the sea. He kept Fenrir close and tied him up with unbreakable chains. Then he kicked Hel out of Asgard, the home of the Norse gods. He sent her to become the queen of the icy underworld.

FACT

The Old Norse word *hel* means "hidden." The underworld remains hidden, just like the dead who are buried beneath

Hel (center) was one of Loki's children, along with the
wolf Fenrir and Jormungand the serpent.

Persephone is the daughter of Zeus, the king of the Greek gods. Zeus was once married to the goddess Themis. But one day, he shocked everyone. He fell in love with his own sister, Demeter! She's the goddess of agriculture and the harvest. Zeus and Demeter had one child together, Persephone. Persephone's parents are both Olympians, so she has more power than the average goddess.

Most historians agree on this version of the story. But another ancient Greek poet wrote that Persephone's mother is Styx. Styx is an Oceanid, which is a **nymph** or a minor nature goddess.

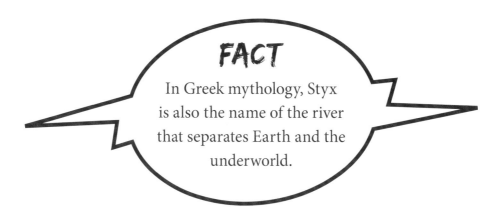

FACT

In Greek mythology, Styx is also the name of the river that separates Earth and the underworld.

Demeter, Greek goddess of the harvest

MIND-BOGGLING STRENGTHS

What is Hel's main strength? She is a strong leader with great authority. In the underworld, she's the boss. Hel judges and decides the fate of the dead souls that come to her. Once her subjects arrive, they must obey her, and she never lets them leave. She has complete control over these souls, and they fear her power.

Hel watches over the souls of the dead in the underworld.

But Hel gets a bad rap. Her world is often described as cold and cheerless. But she isn't really evil. She isn't bloodthirsty, and she doesn't torture most souls. Instead, Hel uses her sense of mercy and justice to watch over the souls in her care. She makes sure they peacefully transfer to the afterlife.

Life in the Afterlife

In Norse culture, dying with honor is important. Warriors who die in battle go to Valhalla and feast with Odin in paradise. Hel receives most of the other souls in the underworld. These are people who may die from old age or sickness. In the underworld, they continue on much like they did while alive—eating, drinking, fighting, and sleeping.

Persephone is skilled at compromising and **adapting** to things. These strengths are seen in the famous myth with Hades. One day, Hades fell in love with Persephone. But he didn't have permission to marry her. That didn't stop him though. He whisked her off to the underworld to marry her anyway.

The nature-loving goddess suddenly had to get used to the dark and gloomy underworld. She adapted and eventually learned to call it home.

Hades kidnapped Persephone on his chariot to live with him in the underworld.

Persephone is much more than just a pretty wife. She shares control over the dead with Hades. She also has **compassion**. When the mortal Psyche begged for help, Persephone gave the woman some of her beauty.

FACT

Persephone's original name was Kore, which means "daughter." After she married Hades, Kore's name changed to Persephone. It means "bringer of death."

Many see Hel as a terrifying goddess. She's in charge of every section in the underworld, including Nastrond. The souls of the wicked dead who committed crimes during life end up there. It's a dark and wet underground cave. Twisted, biting snakes line the walls of Nastrond. And deadly poison trickles down to punish the wicked dead.

But Hel also has a less terrifying side. There's beauty within her role. She represents balance in the life cycle. Old age and death are uncomfortable. But they are natural parts of the cycle of life. Hel helps others respect and accept this cycle, which brings them peace.

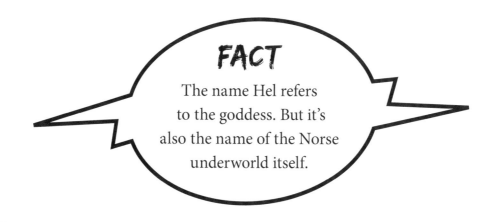

FACT

The name Hel refers to the goddess. But it's also the name of the Norse underworld itself.

Hel sends wicked souls to Nastrond for punishment.

There's more to Persephone than just being the goddess of death. Before marrying Hades, she was the goddess of spring, farming, harvest, and fertility. One of her strengths is her green thumb. She spends a lot of time in nature, planting and taking care of plants and flowers. This connects with her strength of fertility.

Persephone is often seen carrying a **cornucopia.** This container is shaped like a goat's horn. It's usually full of flowers, fruit, and corn.

Persephone also has a strong sense of forgiveness. For example, King Sisyphus once begged Persephone to let him leave the underworld. He longed to return to his wife. Persephone felt sorry for him and let him leave.

Persephone was known as
the goddess of the harvest.

Hel has a special power that no other Norse god has. She can grant life to a dead soul and allow a person to return. For example, when the god Baldur died, she was the only one who could bring him back to life. She promised to let him leave the underworld if everything in existence wept for him.

In addition, Hel is the only one who can send wicked souls to the fierce dragon Nidhogg. Nidhogg torments and punishes these souls. He also chews at the roots of the World Tree, Yggdrasil. This tree is sacred in Norse mythology. It supports the entire universe. Nidhogg's intention is to bring the universe into chaos.

FACT

Hel appears in many movies, TV shows, and video games. For example, she stars in the movie *Thor: Ragnarök* and in Marvel's Thor comic book series.

Norse myths state that the evil serpent Nidhogg bites and torments the souls of the wicked dead.

Persephone has the power to transform people and animals into plants. For example, she once turned the nymph Minthe into a mint plant. She also has the power of **necromancy.** She can call on and communicate with the dead.

Most importantly, Persephone holds power over the seasons. Which means she can also affect the harvest. When Persephone stays in the underworld for half the year, the harvest ends with fall and winter. But when Zeus allows her to return to her mother Demeter, spring and summer bring rebirth and new growth. This shows Persephone's power to give life. Like Hel, she's a source of balance for the cycle of life.

FACT

Persephone appears in Rick Riordan's Percy Jackson and the Olympians book series. She's also featured in the TV series *Hercules: The Legendary Journeys*, among other movies and video games.

When Persephone returns from the underworld, it brings the warmth and new growth of spring to the land.

As the daughter of two Olympians, Persephone is **immortal**. She'll live forever. Most historians believe Hel will die one day at Ragnarök. In Norse mythology, Ragnarök is a great battle at the end of the world. It will end with the death of almost all the Norse gods. However, some historians think Hel will survive the final battle.

Almost all the gods and giants of Norse mythology will die in the final battle of Ragnarök.

Hel and Persephone are similar in some ways. They both hold power in the underworld. They both represent death—and life. Hel's own face and body is half alive and half dead. And Persephone's travels to and from the underworld bring death and new life to the land.

But there is one important difference between these goddesses. Persephone can travel from the underworld to Mount Olympus. Each year, she can go from the land of the dead to the land of the living. But Hel can never leave the underworld.

Greek vs. Norse Afterlife

In both ancient Greek and Norse myths, life never truly ended for most people. It just changed from one state to another. Mortals went to the underworld, where life continued for dead souls. But things were different for Greek and Norse heroes. Greek heroes were rewarded by going to part of the underworld that was a paradise. Norse heroes didn't go to the underworld at all. They were sent to Valhalla, where they enjoy endless feasts and rewards from Odin.

TWO IMPERFECT GODDESSES

Some Norse poets describe Hel as harsh and cruel. She represents the denial of things we enjoy in this world. For example, the poets say her dish is called "Hunger," her knife is called "Famine," and her bed is called "Disease."

Hel is often selfish and lacks **empathy**. One tale describes how the goddess Frigg's son, Baldur, died in an unfair way. Frigg sent a messenger to beg Hel to release Baldur, but Hel didn't care. She only agreed to let him go if every living thing cried over his death. But one giantess, who may have been Loki in disguise, refused to cry. So, Hel kept Baldur in the underworld forever.

The Norse god Hermod (kneeling) was sent
to beg Hel to allow Baldur to return.

Persephone isn't as innocent as she may appear. For example, she's mistress of the Furies. These three wicked creatures punish and take vengeance on some souls in the underworld. Persephone sometimes commands them to torture those souls. She also unleashes the Furies on anyone who dares to curse her name. Others often refer to Persephone as "she who must not be named."

Persephone is also dishonest with her husband Hades. She once fell in love with a handsome mortal man named Adonis. Even though she was married, Persephone fought with Aphrodite to win Adonis's love and attention.

Persephone also has a nasty temper. When Hades paid attention to the nymph Minthe, she grew jealous and angry. Then suddenly, POOF! She turned Minthe into a mint plant and trampled her.

When Persephone first came to the underworld, she knew she couldn't eat any of its food. If she did, she'd remain there forever. But she was weak in the face of temptation. When Hades offered her some pomegranate seeds, she ate them and sealed her fate. She couldn't leave. But later, Zeus made a deal with Hades. Persephone could return to her mother for half the year, which brought new life to the Earth.

Persephone couldn't resist eating some pomegranate seeds in the underworld.

HEL VS. PERSEPHONE AT A GLANCE

Name:	Hel
Goddess of:	the dead and queen of the Norse underworld
Appearance:	half beautiful living woman, half dead with rotting and decaying flesh
Weapons:	a scythe and a sword
Strengths:	sense of leadership and authority, controls many dead souls in the underworld, fair and gracious, doesn't torture souls needlessly, looks after the dead, represents the life cycle and balance
Powers and abilities:	can grant life to a dead soul and allow someone to return to Earth, controls the fierce dragon Nidhogg
Weaknesses:	can be cruel and uncaring, selfish, lacks empathy, her powers over the dead are limited, can't leave the underworld
Symbols:	her watchdog wolf named Garm, anything dying or rotting

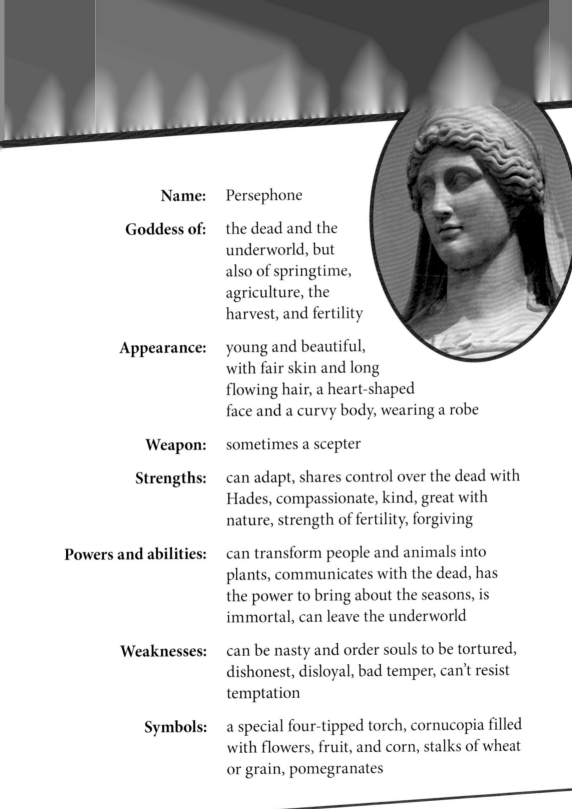

Name:	Persephone
Goddess of:	the dead and the underworld, but also of springtime, agriculture, the harvest, and fertility
Appearance:	young and beautiful, with fair skin and long flowing hair, a heart-shaped face and a curvy body, wearing a robe
Weapon:	sometimes a scepter
Strengths:	can adapt, shares control over the dead with Hades, compassionate, kind, great with nature, strength of fertility, forgiving
Powers and abilities:	can transform people and animals into plants, communicates with the dead, has the power to bring about the seasons, is immortal, can leave the underworld
Weaknesses:	can be nasty and order souls to be tortured, dishonest, disloyal, bad temper, can't resist temptation
Symbols:	a special four-tipped torch, cornucopia filled with flowers, fruit, and corn, stalks of wheat or grain, pomegranates

GLOSSARY

adapt (uh-DAPT)—to change to fit into a new or different environment or situation

compassion (kuhm-PASH-uhn)—concern for the suffering or troubles of others

cornucopia (kor-nuh-KOH-pee-uh)—a horn-shaped basket used to hold food

empathy (EM-puh-thee)—the ability to understand and share the feelings of others

fertility (fer-TIL-ih-tee)—the ability for a person to have a child; the ability of the land to grow crops

immortal (i-MOR-tuhl)—able to live forever

necromancy (NEK-ruh-man-see)—the ability to communicate with the dead

nymph (NIMF)—a mythical maiden or nature goddess often living in a forest or a body of water

pantheon (PAN-thee-on)—all the gods of a certain mythology

prophecy (PROF-uh-see)—a prediction about the future

scythe (SAHYTH)—a tool with a long curved blade at the end of a long pole, usually used for cutting crops

sibling (SIB-ling)—a brother or sister

READ MORE

Alexander, Heather. *A Child's Introduction to Norse Mythology: Odin, Thor, Loki, and Other Viking Gods, Goddesses, Giants, and Monsters*. New York,, USA: Black Dog & Leventhal; 2018.

Loh-Hagan, Virginia. *Medusa vs. Hel*. Ann Arbor, MI: Cherry Lake Publishing, 2020.

Lukidis, Lydia. *Frigg vs. Aphrodite: Battle of the Beauties*. North Mankato, MN: Capstone Press, 2023.

INTERNET SITES

Ancient Greece: Greek Mythology
ducksters.com/history/ancient_greek_mythology.php

Hel
kids.britannica.com/students/article/Hel/314331

Persephone Facts for Kids
kids.kiddle.co/Persephone

INDEX

ABOUT THE AUTHOR

Lydia Lukidis is passionate about science, the ocean, and mythology. She's the author of more than 50 trade and educational books, as well as 31 ebooks. She loves writing STEM titles, such as *Deep, Deep, Down: The Secret Underwater Poetry of the Mariana Trench* (Capstone, 2023) and *The Broken Bees' Nest* (Kane Press, 2019), which was nominated for a Cybils Award. Lydia also helps foster children's literacy and offers writing workshops and author visits in elementary schools.